THIS JOURNAL BELONGS TO

_____

# WHEN GOD CALLS *the* HEART *at Christmas*

## A KEEPSAKE JOURNAL

BELLE
· CITY ·
GIFTS

Belle City Gifts
Savage, Minnesota, USA

Belle City Gifts is an imprint of BroadStreet Publishing Group, LLC.
Broadstreetpublishing.com

WHEN GOD CALLS THE HEART AT CHRISTMAS: *a keepsake journal*
© 2018 by Brian Bird & Michelle Cox

978-1-4245-5730-1

Content compiled and created by Michelle Cox.

Specially marked quotes taken from the *When Calls the Heart* series: Copyright © 2018 by Crown Media Networks, LLC, and used by permission.

Unmarked quotes by Brian Bird and Michelle Cox from *When God Calls the Heart at Christmas: Heartfelt Devotions from Hope Valley*. Used by permission. All rights reserved.

Design by Chris Garborg | garborgdesign.com
Editorial services by Michelle Winger | literallyprecise.com

Printed in China.

18   19   20   21   22   23   24      7   6   5   4   3   2   1

# CELEBRATE CHRISTMAS IN HOPE VALLEY

When Elizabeth Thatcher followed her dream and headed West to become a teacher, one of the things she took with her was her journal. Filled with the memories of her life, it became a treasure for her and for future generations who came to know her through the words she captured there. Now it's your turn. You'll find two parts in this book. The first section includes space for you to journal, to reflect, to list your prayer requests, or to do whatever else God places on your heart.

Christmas was a special time for the citizens of Hope Valley as it is for us today, so the second section is the keepsake part of the journal where you can record the precious memories with your family this Christmas. We know from experience that your journal will become priceless as the years go by.

If you haven't discovered the companion devotional book, *When God Calls the Heart at Christmas: Heartfelt Devotions from Hope Valley*, it's written by inspirational writer Michelle Cox and Brian Bird, the executive producer and co-creator of the *When Calls the Heart* television series on which the devotional is based.

*When God Calls the Heart at Christmas* contains twenty-five devotions that illuminate the Christmas God-moments from the fictional 1910 mining town of Hope Valley, delicious holiday recipes your family can enjoy, and stories that will touch your heart or make you laugh (many of them submitted by the Hearties—the fans of the show). These devotions, taken from episodes of *When Calls the Heart*, will encourage and inspire you as you enjoy this holy season.

We hope you'll make good use of your *When God Calls the Heart Journal* and that you'll take time to capture your family's Christmas moments. We're confident that by the time you fill in the last beautiful page, you'll have learned what the citizens of Hope Valley always do. When God calls your heart at Christmas, you can expect a celebration.

Merry Christmas,

Brian Bird and Michelle Cox

_____

_____

_____

_____

_____

_____

_____

_____

_____

_____

_____

_____

_____

_____

_____

_____

_____

_____

_____

_____

_____

The good news is that
God's gifts never disappoint.

Don't let the Scrooges in your life
keep you from practicing compassion.

Send someone to me this Christmas
who needs to hear about you. Show me
how to bear their burdens with them,
so I can lighten their load.

Instead of gifting him with what he
deserved, Abigail baked some of her
special scones and sent the gift to Henry.

Love is patient, love is kind. It does not
envy, it does not boast, it is not proud.
It does not dishonor others, it is not
self-seeking, it is not easily angered,
it keeps no record of wrongs.

1 CORINTHIANS 13: 4–5 NIV

The God who made the universe—who loves
the world so much that He sent His Son
to sacrifice Himself for our wrongs—cares
about the smallest details of our lives.

_____
_____
_____
_____
_____
_____
_____
_____
_____
_____
_____
_____
_____
_____
_____
_____
_____
_____
_____
_____
_____
_____
_____
_____

Do you need to come home to God today? A warm welcome is waiting for you and it would be the perfect Christmas gift to Him.

Return to the Lord your God,

for he is gracious and compassionate,

slow to anger and abounding in love.

JOEL 2:13 NIV

For those who have no experience
with church or the Bible, people of
faith may be the only example of true
hospitality they will ever see.

When we extend generosity to others,
we always end up blessed as well
because hospitality is the gift that
always gives back double.

Show hospitality to one another
without grumbling.

1 PETER 4:9 ESV

_____
_____
_____
_____
_____
_____
_____
_____
_____
_____
_____
_____
_____
_____
_____
_____
_____
_____
_____
_____
_____
_____
_____
_____

Lord, make my home a place where
people will feel a warm welcome this
Christmas—where their hearts will
heal, and where they will sense your
presence in every room.

The holidays can be an especially painful
time for fractured relationships. Making
amends is the best medicine for the
hurt we do to others—and even better
medicine for our own wounded hearts.

Dr. Carson Shepherd's Christmas efforts to break through to Myra McCormick's frosty heart took a while. But once the thaw started, an obvious change occurred.

_____

_____

_____

_____

_____

_____

_____

_____

_____

_____

_____

_____

_____

_____

_____

_____

_____

_____

_____

Bear with each other and forgive one
another if any of you has a grievance
against someone. Forgive as the Lord
forgave you. And over all these virtues
put on love, which binds them all
together in perfect unity.

COLOSSIANS 3:13-14 NIV

_____

_____

_____

_____

_____

_____

_____

_____

_____

_____

_____

_____

_____

_____

_____

_____

_____

_____

_____

_____

_____

_____

_____

At Christmas God gave up His beloved
Son because He loved us so much.
To Him, we were worth the sacrifice.

_____

_____

_____

_____

_____

_____

_____

_____

_____

_____

_____

_____

_____

_____

_____

_____

_____

_____

_____

You probably have many friends you love
dearly—but would you give up one of your
children for them? It would be such an
unfair choice for any of us to have to make,
and yet God made that choice for us.
Unconditional love wrapped in swaddling
clothes. Because He thought we were worth it.

_____

_____

_____

_____

_____

_____

_____

_____

_____

_____

_____

_____

_____

_____

_____

_____

_____

_____

_____

_____

_____

_____

_____

_____

"For God so loved the world that
he gave his one and only Son, that
whoever believes in him shall not
perish but have eternal life."

JOHN 3:16 NIV

_____

_____

_____

_____

_____

_____

_____

_____

_____

_____

_____

_____

_____

_____

_____

_____

_____

_____

Have you ever felt so much gratitude to God
that you wanted to offer something back to
Him? God already has everything He needs.
But the one thing He treasures above all is
that you love Him, not out of obligation or
guilt, but just because you do. That's the one
gift that's guaranteed to touch His heart.

_____
_____
_____
_____
_____
_____
_____
_____
_____
_____
_____
_____
_____
_____
_____
_____
_____
_____
_____
_____
_____
_____
_____
_____
_____

"Love the Lord your God with all your
heart and with all your soul and with all
your mind and with all your strength."

MARK 12:30 NIV

_____

_____

_____

_____

_____

_____

_____

_____

_____

_____

_____

_____

_____

_____

_____

_____

_____

_____

_____

_____

Lord, I so want to do something this
Christmas to show you how much I
appreciate your blessings and how much I
love you. But no gift is good enough for
that. All I have to bring you is my heart.

_____
_____
_____
_____
_____
_____
_____
_____
_____
_____
_____
_____
_____
_____
_____
_____
_____
_____
_____
_____
_____
_____
_____
_____

Music is an important part of Christmas.
It began with the choir of angels who
serenaded shepherds in a field on
the night Jesus was born.

Praise the Lord.

How good it is to sing praises to our God,

how pleasant and fitting to praise him!

PSALM 147:1 NIV

---
_____
_____
_____
_____
_____
_____
_____
_____
_____
_____
_____
_____
_____
_____
_____
_____
_____
_____
_____
_____
_____

Joseph and Mary were forced on a dusty
road trip as birth pangs began to wrack
Mary's body. Instead of a beautifully-
crafted crib, their new son would be placed
into a lowly stable manger—a humble
beginning and beautiful reminder that
God's love is available to all.

The question for us is,
"How do we welcome Him?"

_____

_____

_____

_____

_____

_____

_____

_____

_____

_____

_____

_____

_____

_____

_____

_____

_____

_____

_____

_____

_____

_____

_____

Now when Jesus returned, the crowd
welcomed him, for they were all
waiting for him.

LUKE 8:40 ESV

_____

_____

_____

_____

_____

_____

_____

_____

_____

_____

_____

_____

_____

_____

_____

_____

_____

_____

_____

_____

_____

_____

Sometimes we wish for things that seem
impossible: hopes and dreams that we really
want to accomplish, but there are so many
obstacles in the way that it looks hopeless.

God doesn't expect perfection. He knows how hard it is to get it all right in this world. That's exactly why that baby in the manger came—He makes everything right if we will just offer our past to Him and ask for a Henry Gowen do-over.

_____

_____

_____

_____

_____

_____

_____

_____

_____

_____

_____

_____

_____

_____

_____

_____

_____

_____

_____

_____

_____

_____

_____

_____

Elizabeth wondered what they could do
to help, but then Jack had the answer,
"We can pray for a miracle."

_____

_____

_____

_____

_____

_____

_____

_____

_____

_____

_____

_____

_____

_____

_____

_____

_____

_____

_____

_____

Those are difficult times when we love folks
whose hearts are heavy and we don't know
how to help. But we can tell them about
our faithful God. And then we can pray
for a miracle—because God is still in the
miracle-working business today.

_____

_____

_____

_____

_____

_____

_____

_____

_____

_____

_____

_____

_____

_____

_____

_____

_____

_____

_____

_____

_____

Maybe the miracle is actually you.
God can use you as His hands and
feet in the life of your friend or
loved one this Christmas.

Jesus looked at them and said,
"With man this is impossible, but
with God all things are possible."

MATTHEW 19:26 ESV

"Being away from home makes you
grateful for the things you left behind."

—JACK THORNTON

_____

_____

_____

_____

_____

_____

_____

_____

_____

_____

_____

_____

_____

_____

_____

_____

_____

_____

_____

_____

Thank you, God, for the special time of
Christmas. For the priceless gift of your
Son. And for the wonderful memories we
make as we celebrate His birth.

_____
_____
_____
_____
_____
_____
_____
_____
_____
_____
_____
_____
_____
_____
_____
_____
_____
_____
_____
_____

God is never challenged by our
circumstances and He will be enough for
whatever we face. Because we have that
hope, we can go to Him in prayer about
everything—at Christmas, or any other
day of the year—knowing that nothing is
impossible for Him.

_____

_____

_____

_____

_____

_____

_____

_____

_____

_____

_____

_____

_____

_____

_____

_____

_____

_____

_____

_____

_____

_____

Immanuel is the Hebrew word for
"Messiah," but it also means "God with
us." And He is... forever and always.

_____

_____

_____

_____

_____

_____

_____

_____

_____

_____

_____

_____

_____

_____

_____

_____

_____

_____

_____

_____

_____

"For to us a child is born, to us a son
is given, and the government will be
on his shoulders. And he will be called
Wonderful Counselor, Mighty God,
Everlasting Father, Prince of Peace."

ISAIAH 9:6 NIV

----------------------------------------

----------------------------------------

----------------------------------------

----------------------------------------

----------------------------------------

----------------------------------------

----------------------------------------

----------------------------------------

----------------------------------------

----------------------------------------

----------------------------------------

----------------------------------------

----------------------------------------

----------------------------------------

----------------------------------------

----------------------------------------

----------------------------------------

----------------------------------------

----------------------------------------

"I've been blessed to spend these last few
days with Jack. Tonight will be our best
Christmas Eve ever... until he has to leave
again. It will be a challenge not to show
my concerns about his safety, so I have to
remember that God has a plan—
and we have to trust it."

—ELIZABETH THATCHER

_____

_____

_____

_____

_____

_____

_____

_____

_____

_____

_____

_____

_____

_____

_____

_____

_____

_____

_____

_____

Have you ever experienced circumstances
at Christmastime that distressed you or
caused you sadness? As Elizabeth learned,
you can choose to cling to the One who
gives us hope. And you can follow her
example because of one certain truth:
God is faithful.

_____
_____
_____
_____
_____
_____
_____
_____
_____
_____
_____
_____
_____
_____
_____
_____
_____
_____
_____
_____
_____
_____
_____
_____

Those who know Your name
will put their trust in You;
For You, Lord, have not forsaken
those who seek You.

PSALM 9:10 NKJV

_____

_____

_____

_____

_____

_____

_____

_____

_____

_____

_____

_____

_____

_____

_____

_____

_____

Hope Valley's citizens lined the street,
talking with their neighbors, waving as
their friends passed by on the floats, and
laughing as the children dove to grab
the candy that was thrown to the crowd.
And all alone, Henry Gowen stood in the
doorway of the jail, intently watching the
proceedings with a wistful look on his face.

Sometimes we forget that people are
watching us. They take in how we live
our lives, the examples we set, and
whether we are even aware of them.
And the scary truth is that we might be
the only example of forgiveness and
generosity that they will ever see.

Keep an eye open this Christmas for
someone who has their eye on you. And
remember to stay so close to God that when
others look at you, they see Him instead.

_____

_____

_____

_____

_____

_____

_____

_____

_____

_____

_____

_____

_____

_____

_____

_____

_____

_____

_____

_____

_____

_____

_____

_____

"Let your light so shine before men,
that they may see your good works and
glorify your Father in heaven."

MATTHEW 5:16 NKJV

_____

_____

_____

_____

_____

_____

_____

_____

_____

_____

_____

_____

_____

_____

_____

_____

_____

_____

_____

_____

Are we missing what Christmas is all about?
Are we ignoring the One whom the season
is all about? Shouldn't we be pondering the
story of His birth and how that changes the
universe and our lives forever?

Don't forget to make time this Christmas
to worship the Savior, to sing His praises,
and to express your thanks for the most
amazing gift ever given.

"Be still, and know that I am God;
I will be exalted among the nations,
I will be exalted in the earth!"

PSALM 46:10 NKJV

_____

_____

_____

_____

_____

_____

_____

_____

_____

_____

_____

_____

_____

_____

_____

_____

_____

_____

_____

_____

_____

The God of the universe wants to be close
to us. He wants to know our hearts. And
this special time of the year is the perfect
time to come to Him with fresh, new
anticipation as we seek to know His heart.

_____

_____

_____

_____

_____

_____

_____

_____

_____

_____

_____

_____

_____

_____

_____

_____

_____

_____

_____

_____

_____

_____

_____

"You will seek Me and find Me, when you

search for Me with all your heart."

JEREMIAH 29:13 NKJV

---
---
---
---
---
---
---
---
---
---
---
---
---
---
---
---
---
---
---
---
---
---

Christmas is a perfect time to remember
God's faithfulness in the past, so that we can
be confident today, and know just how much
He will love and care for us tomorrow.

_____

_____

_____

_____

_____

_____

_____

_____

_____

_____

_____

_____

_____

_____

_____

_____

_____

_____

_____

_____

_____

_____

"Remember the things I have done in the past.

For I alone am God!

I am God, and there is none like me."

ISAIAH 46:9 NLT

Peddler Sam gently reminded
Pastor Frank that a star led the Wise
Men to Bethlehem—his hint that
God would lead Frank.

_____

_____

_____

_____

_____

_____

_____

_____

_____

_____

_____

_____

_____

_____

_____

_____

_____

_____

_____

_____

_____

_____

Are you the lost sheep God's searching
for today? Don't run from Him. Run to
Him—and there will be great rejoicing as
the Shepherd gathers you into the safety
of His loving arms.

_____

_____

_____

_____

_____

_____

_____

_____

_____

_____

_____

_____

_____

_____

_____

_____

_____

_____

_____

_____

_____

_____

"What man of you, having a hundred
sheep, if he loses one of them, does not
leave the ninety-nine in the wilderness,
and go after the one which is lost until he
finds it? And when he has found it, he
lays it on his shoulders, rejoicing."

LUKE 15:4–5 NKJV

---

---

---

---

---

---

---

---

---

---

---

---

---

---

---

---

---

---

"It's hard to follow the greatest story ever told, so I won't even try—but I do want to remind everyone that the greatest gift we receive is God's love. The greatest gift that we give is the love we have for one another."

—PASTOR FRANK

There's no greater story than the birth
of that baby in Bethlehem. God's love is
a priceless gift—and He doesn't want us
to keep that news to ourselves.

That is the great take-away of Christmas
for all of us: God first loved us, so that
in turn we can love each other.

_____

_____

_____

_____

_____

_____

_____

_____

_____

_____

_____

_____

_____

_____

_____

_____

_____

_____

_____

There comes a time when we need to put
away the frivolous, and figure out how to
be faithful when the lights aren't flickering
and the egg nog isn't flowing—because the
purpose of Christmas isn't just a one-day
event—it's for eternity.

_____

_____

_____

_____

_____

_____

_____

_____

_____

_____

_____

_____

_____

_____

_____

_____

_____

_____

_____

_____

Let's take the meaning of Christmas with
us into the new year. Let's make this the
year we draw closer to Him, where we listen
for His whispers, where we make ourselves
available for whatever He asks, and where
we share His story with a world that
desperately needs to hear it.

_____

_____

_____

_____

_____

_____

_____

_____

_____

_____

_____

_____

_____

_____

_____

_____

_____

_____

_____

_____

_____

_____

_____

Lord, this is the day we commemorate
your birth, but I'm the one who
received the best gift.

# OUR CHRISTMAS KEEPSAKE JOURNAL

This book contains the Christmas memories

of the _____ family.

*Christmas*

20____

# WHY CHRISTMAS IS
# SPECIAL TO OUR FAMILY

Christmas is exceptional for so many reasons. This year, let your family members tell why Christmas is special to them. Be sure to put their names at the beginning of the lines where they'll write. If some of the children haven't started school yet, ask them why they love Christmas and jot their thoughts down for them. A few prompts might include "Christmas is special to me because…" or "I love Christmas because…" or "My favorite part of Christmas is…." Years from now, this will be a priceless treasure for your family.

_____

_____

_____

_____

_____

_____

_____

_____

_____

_____

_____

_____

_____

_____

_____

_____

_____

_____

_____

# FAVORITE FAMILY
# CHRISTMAS TRADITIONS

What are your favorite family Christmas traditions and why are they special to you? Do you bake cookies together each year? Do you purchase a special ornament for each family member? Do you read the Christmas story together every Christmas Eve? Does the entire family watch a certain Christmas movie? Do you make tree-shaped pancakes or cinnamon rolls on Christmas morning? Use your imagination and establish your own unique family traditions.

_____

_____

_____

_____

_____

_____

_____

_____

_____

_____

_____

_____

_____

_____

_____

_____

_____

_____

# GIFTS OF SERVICE
# THIS CHRISTMAS

What gifts of service did you do this Christmas in honor of the birth
of Jesus? Here are some ideas to help you get started: volunteer
at a shelter, collect coats and gloves for the homeless, help a single
parent, have young children color pictures for nursing home
residents, provide gifts for someone whose finances are tight,
help with your church Christmas play, bake cookies and take them
to elderly neighbors.

_____

_____

_____

_____

_____

_____

_____

_____

_____

_____

_____

_____

_____

_____

_____

_____

_____

_____

# THE HISTORY OF OUR ORNAMENTS AND DECORATIONS

Write down the history of your Christmas ornaments and decorations. Do you have heirloom ornaments or decorations that belonged to your parents or grandparents? Is there a decoration with sentimental significance? Do you buy special ornaments for each child? Did the kids make you an ornament or decoration, or did you make some together as a family? Did you buy commemorative ornaments on a family trip or purchase them for a special occasion? Capture the stories of your treasures for your children and grandchildren.

_____

_____

_____

_____

_____

_____

_____

_____

_____

_____

_____

_____

_____

_____

_____

_____

_____

_____

_____

_____

# KEEPING CHRIST
# IN CHRISTMAS

What was your favorite faith-filled moment this Christmas? Were there instances that brought tears to your eyes? Did a Christmas play or carol touch your soul? How did this special time of the year bless your heart?

# OUR CHRISTMAS
# WISH LISTS

What's on your Christmas wish list this year? Have every family member jot their lists down on these pages. Be sure to include names next to the lists. Years from now, you'll love looking back to see what everyone wanted (and you'll probably be surprised to see how many of those products are no longer made).

_____

_____

_____

_____

_____

_____

_____

_____

_____

_____

_____

_____

_____

_____

_____

_____

_____

_____

_____

_____

_____

_____

# OUR CHILDHOOD
# CHRISTMAS MEMORIES

Moms and dads, sometimes we forget to share our own stories with
our children and grandchildren. What was your best Christmas
memory from your childhood? What were the holidays like at your
house when you were growing up? What humorous things happened at
Christmas? What were your favorite holiday foods that your parents or
grandparents made? Capture those memories here.

_____

_____

_____

_____

_____

_____

_____

_____

_____

_____

_____

_____

_____

_____

_____

_____

_____

_____

_____

_____

# OUR FAVORITE GIFTS

What is your favorite gift that you received this Christmas?
Why? What is your favorite gift you gave this Christmas?
Why? Have each family member respond to these questions
and write their answers here.

_____

_____

_____

_____

_____

_____

_____

_____

_____

_____

_____

_____

_____

_____

_____

_____

_____

_____

_____

_____

_____

_____

# OUR HOLIDAY ACTIVITIES

Here's the place to preserve the memories of your holiday activities.
Where did you go this Christmas? Did you take a tour of homes?
Did you go to see a live nativity or to hear a singing Christmas tree?
Did you see a Christmas movie? Did you go to a special church
service? Did you host fun events for your kids or with family and
friends? Capture all those moments here.

_____

_____

_____

_____

_____

_____

_____

_____

_____

_____

_____

_____

_____

_____

_____

_____

_____

_____

_____

_____

_____

# OUR CHRISTMAS EVE
# AND CHRISTMAS DAY

Here's the place to record the events of both days and the excitement of the children—and the big kids. What did you have for breakfast and dinner? Does your family open gifts on Christmas Eve or Christmas Day? Did you stay at home or did you travel to spend Christmas with family or friends? Did you read the Christmas story? Include a history of the guests who shared your Christmas dinner, the menu, table decorations, etc. Did something poignant or funny happen? Did family or friends drop by?

_____

_____

_____

_____

_____

_____

_____

_____

_____

_____

_____

_____

_____

_____

_____

_____

_____

_____

# MEMORIES
# TO TREASURE

What are your favorite memories from this Christmas? Here's the place to preserve those wonderful moments that happen throughout the Christmas season and at each holiday get-together. Make sure each family member records their memories. Did you host a party? What were the funny moments? What were the memorable moments that happened this year? What cute things did a child say or do?

_____

_____

_____

_____

_____

_____

_____

_____

_____

_____

_____

_____

_____

_____

_____

_____

_____

_____

_____

_____

# OUR FAVORITE CHRISTMAS FOODS AND RECIPES

Here's space to preserve your favorite family holiday recipes. Is this an old family recipe? Is this a new treat? Is this the must-have item every year or you won't feel like it's Christmas? Do you have a certain cookie recipe that you make together every year? Answer those questions and jot down those recipes to preserve them for future generations. Don't forget to share the history of the recipes and any other interesting tidbits.

_____

_____

_____

_____

_____

_____

_____

_____

_____

_____

_____

_____

_____

_____

_____

_____

_____

_____

# ODDS AND ENDS

Use these pages for the items that don't fit one of the other sections or to jot down information that will be helpful when the next holiday season arrives—things like favorite businesses or websites for Christmas shopping, gift ideas for next year, reminders that you purchased twenty-five rolls of gift wrap at after-Christmas sales, etc.

_____

_____

_____

_____

_____

_____

_____

_____

_____

_____

_____

_____

_____

_____

_____

_____

_____

_____

_____

_____

# ALWAYS REMEMBER

What are the cherished moments, life experiences, and lessons you hope your children and grandchildren will remember about holiday times with you? This is the place to share your heart.

_____

_____

_____

_____

_____

_____

_____

_____

_____

_____

_____

_____

_____

_____

_____

_____

_____

_____

_____

_____

_____

_____

_____

# FINDING CHRIST IN CHRISTMAS

Did you know that familiar Christmas moments can also provide some spiritual lessons if we'll just look for the God-moments in them?

- Candles cast a bright light in our houses—and we can be a light in a dark world that needs to hear about God.
- Candy canes provide a delicious sweetness—and our lives should show the sweetness of God to those with whom we come in contact.
- Gifts are always a joy—and they're a great reminder that we need to share the gift of God's love to others.
- The Christmas tree is a beautiful symbol of the One who was nailed to a tree because He loves us so much.
- Christmas cards can remind us to be encouragers and also to pray for those who sent the cards to us.
- Wish lists are fun at any age. This year, what if we made our wish lists of big dreams to do for God?
- Sleigh rides take us on adventures—and they're reminders that we should be willing to go wherever God sends us... even when those adventures take us out of our comfort zones.
- Ornaments are beautiful decorations—and our lives can be beautiful reflections of God's grace and mercy.
- Everyone loves to receive some delicious Christmas goodies— and they can be great prompts to make us think about God's sweet blessings to us.
- Christmas carols provide the perfect opportunity for us to worship the One who is the reason for the season.
- Our nativity sets are great reminders to share God's story— because not everyone has heard it.
- A white Christmas with its pristine snow is a beautiful symbol of how we should aim for a heart that is pure before God.
- Christmas shopping can help us think about having a giving spirit. There are people all around us who can use a helping hand.

- A new Christmas outfit is a reminder to make sure that our inward beauty outshines our outward beauty.
- Setting up a model Christmas village reminds us to reach out to our neighbors and town to see how we can be a blessing.
- Children are great reminders to look for joy—and the best joy is found in God.
- The garland is an awesome symbol of God's grace that wraps around our hearts and lives.
- And our Christmas dinner is a reminder to be hospitable to others. It's a wonderful time to invite folks who might otherwise be alone through the holidays.

Where else can you discover God in your Christmas celebrations this year? Look for those God-moments in your everyday life and share them with your family, friends, and others.